THE POLITICS OF THE CIVIL WAR

THE POLITICS OF THE CIVIL WAR

MASON CREST

Mason Crest
450 Parkway Drive, Suite D
Broomall, PA 19008
www.masoncrest.com

Library of Congress Cataloging-in-Publication Data

Cataloging-in-Publication Data on file with the Library of Congress.

Printed and bound in the United States of America.

First printing
9 8 7 6 5 4 3 2 1

ISBN: 978-1-4222-3885-1
Series ISBN: 978-1-4222-3881-3
ebook ISBN: 978-1-4222-7895-6
ebook series ISBN: 978-1-4222-7891-8

Produced by Regency House Publishing Limited
The Manor House
High Street
Buntingford
Hertfordshire
SG9 9AB
United Kingdom

www.regencyhousepublishing.com

Text copyright © 2018 Regency House Publishing Limited/Jonathan Sutherland and Diane Canwell

PAGE 2: General Ulysses S. Grant.

PAGE 3: President Abraham Lincoln visiting Union army troops at City Point, Virginia, 1865
Lithograph from a painting by Gustav Bartsch.

RIGHT: Frederick Douglass (1818–1895), African American abolitionist, writer, and statesman.

PAGE 6: African American "contrabands" (escaped slaves), at Foller's house, Cumberland Landing, Virginia.

CONTENTS

KEY ICONS TO LOOK FOR:

 Words to Understand: These words with their easy-to-understand definitions will increase the reader's understanding of the text, while building vocabulary skills.

 Sidebars: This boxed material within the main text allows readers to build knowledge, gain insights, explore possibilities, and broaden their perspectives by weaving together additional information to provide realistic and holistic perspectives.

 Educational Videos: Readers can view videos by scanning our QR codes, providing them with additional content to supplement the text. Examples include news coverage, moments in history, speeches, iconic sports moments, and much more!

 Text-Dependent Questions: These questions send the reader back to the text for more careful attention to the evidence presented here.

 Research Projects: Readers are pointed toward areas of further inquiry connected to each chapter. Suggestions are provided for projects that encourage deeper research and analysis.

 Series Glossary of Key Terms: This back-of-the-book glossary contains terminology used throughout the series. Words found here increase the reader's ability to read and comprehend high-level books and articles in this field.

The Pennsylvania State Memorial is a monument in Gettysburg National Military Park that commemorates the 34,530 Pennsylvania soldiers who fought in the Battle of Gettysburg.

Lincoln Memorial

The grand Lincoln Memorial is an American national monument built to honor the 16th President of the United States, Abraham Lincoln. It was designed by Henry Bacon, a New York architect. He had spent time studying in Europe where he was influenced and inspired by ancient Greek architecture. It was based on the architecture of a Greek temple. There are 36 Doric columns, each one representing one state of the U.S. at the date of President Lincoln's death.

The memorial contains a large seated sculpture of Abraham Lincoln. The nineteen-foot tall statue of Abraham Lincoln was designed by Daniel Chester French who was a leading sculptor from Massachusetts. The marble statue was carved in white Georgia marble by the Piccirilli brothers. The interior murals were painted by Jules Guerin. Ernest C. Bairstow created the exterior details with carvings by Evelyn Beatrice Longman. The memorial is inscribed with Lincoln's famous speech, "The Gettysburg Address." The words of the speech are etched into the wall to inspire all Americans just as it did in 1863. To the right is the entire Second Inaugural Address, given by Lincoln in March 1865. The memorial itself is 190 feet long, 119 feet wide, and almost 100 feet high. It took 8 years to complete from 1914–1922.

At its most basic level the Lincoln Memorial symbolizes the idea of Freedom. The Lincoln Memorial is often used as a gathering place for protests and political rallies. The Memorial has become a symbolically sacred venue especially for the Civil Rights movement. On August 28, 1963, the memorial grounds were the site of the *March on Washington for Jobs and Freedom*, which proved to the high point of the *American Civil Rights Movement*. It is estimated that approximately 250,000 people came to the event, where they heard Martin Luther King, Jr. deliver his historic speech "*I have a Dream.*" King's speech, with its language of patriotism and its evocation of Lincoln's Gettysburg Address, was meant to match the symbolism of the Lincoln Memorial as a monument to national unity.

The Lincoln Memorial is located on the western end of the National Mall in Washington, D.C., across from the Washington Monument, and towers over the Reflecting Pool. The memorial is maintained by the U.S. National Park Service, and receives approximately 8 million visitors each year. It is open 24 hours a day and is free to all visitors.

Chapter One
POLITICS OF THE NORTH AND SOUTH

Many pondered the question as to why the great democratic institution of the United States appeared to have failed. Ever since the 1820s it seemed as though the more powerful North had been unable to rein in the South. Even bigger federations of states and territories had been able to cope with change far better than the

Words to Understand

Democrat: A supporter of the Democratic Party in the U.S.

Martial Law: Law applied by a military authority.

Republican: A supporter of the Republican Party in the U.S.

United States; people looked at the Roman and British Empires and wondered why the United States had so singularly failed to remain a cohesive unit. What seemed to be the answer was the fact that most of the rest of the world had abolished slavery, or had at least restricted it, but the United States had expanded it instead. Buchanan's ditherings in the last months of his presidency had not helped; in fact he had

OPPOSITE: President Lincoln (left) and General George B. McClellan in the general's tent during the Battle of Antietam in 1862.

ABOVE: President Abraham Lincoln (1809–65), the 16th president of the United States.

RIGHT: James Buchanan.

failed to act as the Southern states threatened secession before taking the ultimate step. Few truly believed that Abraham Lincoln was up to the job and many thought he would follow Buchanan in his failure.

In the early months of the Civil War all Lincoln could do was hope the Union would survive. Disastrous defeats piled huge pressure on him as each successive commanding general failed him in the field. But as this was happening, the political system continued to operate. There were congressional, state and local elections in 1862 and a

presidential election in 1864. The continuation of politics as usual was vital to the stability of the United States, in that democracy was seen to be still working.

Some Democrats in the North were seen as guilty by association with the secessionists. Many of them harbored hopes that the war would prove so ruinous for the North that an armistice would take place and a separate Confederacy would coexist alongside what remained of the Union. For some time they believed that all the Confederacy had to do was endure the war; it would be the North that would capitulate, seeking to end the conflict it was not winning. To this end, every expenditure connected with the war was challenged by the Democrats, in the hope of wearing the Republicans down.

They also challenged arrests of those considered to be disloyal to the Union, the Emancipation Proclamation, and the recruitment

ABOVE: Band of the 107th U.S. Colored Infantry at Fort Corcoran, Arlington, Virginia.

OPPOSITE: General McClellan and his wife.

OVERLEAF: The Cavalry Charge of Lt. Henry B. Hidden, 1862
Victor Nehlig (1830–1909).
Oil on canvas.

of black soldiers from 1862. The Democrats would find an able and vociferous leader in General McClellan, when he was forced out of the army.

Slowly, public opinion began to turn in favour of emancipation and eventually emancipation and Union victory became synonymous, much to the credit of Lincoln. He had held the Republicans together, acted with sensitivity, and had never tried to coerce his colleagues into making

decisions they were not yet ready to contemplate.

When he came to power in 1861 it was clear that he hated slavery, but he was not, as yet, an abolitionist. He believed the Constitution would deal with slavery, by curtailing its spread while working for its extinction. Above all, Lincoln believed that the light but steady hand of Washington would guide the people and the states. He wanted the people to be independent and for the states to be strong, while acting together as a nation. Such

was Lincoln's view of democracy that his vision attracted the financial genius of Secretary of the Treasury, Salmon P. Chase, the ultimate administrator, Secretary of War, Edwin M. Stanton, and influential abolitionists such as Frederick Douglass.

Lincoln used to liken his government and army to a wagon with four different teams of horses. In the lead team were the radical Republicans, desperate to gain emancipation and to crush the Confederacy. In the next were the more moderate Republicans,

ABOVE: General Sherman and his Staff.

OPPOSITE LEFT: General Robert E. Lee.

who sometimes sped ahead with the radicals and at other times stopped altogether. As his government was a coalition, the third contained Democrats, who simply moved towards their goal of a reformed Union with the South. The final team comprised the old-fashioned **Democrats**, who did everything to hinder the

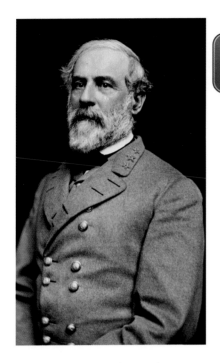

progress of the Union and even reverse its course. Added to these four disparate groups were the Copperheads – extreme anti-war Democrats – who wanted peace on any terms.

The Copperheads were particularly active in Illinois, Indiana, and Ohio. Lincoln had his own subtle way of dealing with them: when Clement Vallandigham, an Ohio Congressman, violated a general order forbidding declarations of sympathy towards the Confederacy in 1863, he was arrested and Lincoln banished him from the Union. He was sent through the front lines to the Confederacy and from there to Canada, to return in 1864 with his tail between his legs.

The **Republican** majority in the House of Representatives was cut from 35 to 18 as a result of the

ALLAN J. PINKERTON (1819–1884)

Allan Pinkerton was born on August 25, 1819 in Glasgow, Scotland. In 1842 he emigrated to the United States where he became interested in detective work and subsequently became the founder of a famous private detective agency, The Pinkerton National Detective Agency. Pinkerton's agency thwarted a plot aimed to assassinate President-elect Abraham Lincoln and, working for the Union during the Civil War, he headed a group whose purpose was to obtain military information in the Southern States. After he retired, he wrote three books about his experiences. Allan Pinkerton died in 1884. It has been reported that Pinkerton slipped while out walking and bit his tongue resulting in gangrene, although other reports suggest other causes of death. Pinkerton is buried in Graceland Cemetery, Chicago, Illinois. Following his death, his agency continued to operate and became a major force against the labor moment in the U.S. and Canada.

1862 elections, which did not deter Lincoln from taking the long-term view. He sacked General McClellan and announced a two-part Emancipation Proclamation. The first was that all slaves would be permanently freed in all areas of the Confederacy that had not already returned to Federal control by January 1, 1863. The second part, after the deadline had been passed, was to authorize the Provost Marshall General of the Union army, under the Conscription Act of March 1863, to begin enrolling both black and white men.

Fighting on what appeared to be an anti-war platform, the Democrats, led by the former General McClellan, were crushed by Lincoln in the 1864 presidential election. In fact, Lincoln's share of the popular vote was 15 percent more than it had been in 1860. He

was the first president to have been re-elected since Jackson.

The politics of the Confederate States of America is more difficult to express. There was no long-term vision of the future, since it was their desire to preserve their own way of life, which they regarded as threatened by the dominance of the North and the government in Washington. The basis upon

LEFT: Edwin M. Stanton, President Lincoln's Secretary of War.

ABOVE: Salmon P. Chase.

RIGHT: Alexander H. Stephens, vice president of the Confederate states.

OPPOSITE: President Lincoln with Allan Pinkerton (left) and Major General John A. McClernand at Antietam.

which they had seceded and fought the Civil War was how they interpreted the contract signed back in 1789. The Federal government formed at that time was intended to secure the interests of the member states, because they felt the Union had failed. Consequently, they felt free to declare the contract void and regain their independence.

The Confederate Constitution was essentially conservationist and nationalistic, which very much reflected the Constitution of the old Union. A Confederate president could serve for six years but not seek re-election. He could request expenditure, but it would have to be agreed by Congress. On March 21, 1861, Vice President Alexander H. Stephens confirmed that slavery was the "cornerstone" of the Confederacy.

ABOVE: Sherman and his men in Atlanta, Georgia.

LEFT: The Copperhead Plan for Subjugating the South
The cartoon shows a delegation of Copperheads entreating a Southerner to return to the Union.

OPPOSITE: Officers of the Army of the Potomac in their winter quarters at Brandy Station.

Jefferson Davis had been chosen as Confederate president for his moderate views, having all the necessary credentials to make him the ideal choice. He was a West Point graduate, a planter, a congressman, a secretary of war and a senator. His major shortcomings were his inability to delegate, his tendency to hold grudges, and his misplaced loyalty to people who were liabilities to the cause. Both Davis and Stephens were selected and inaugurated with indecent speed (two weeks). Davis set about choosing his cabinet, taking men from every original Confederate state. He also built up a selection of advisers, on whose opinion he could rely.

As mobilization got under way, Arkansas, North Carolina, Tennessee, and Virginia joined the Confederacy and it seemed for a while that Kentucky, Maryland, and Missouri would follow suit. It was decided to reward Virginia for its allegiance to the South by placing the Confederate capital in Richmond.

It soon became clear, however, that the Confederacy needed central control; for example, the states needed to hang on to their militia troops, rather than releasing them to serve in Confederate freed armies.

From early on it had been obvious that the victories of 1861 would not be enough to defeat the Union. Davis and the Confederacy had hoped for a short, decisive war, but the Union was in for the longer haul. Moreover, it had access to greater resources and could strike anywhere. In the spring of 1862 Davis decided he would declare **martial law**, suspend trial by jury, and introduce conscription. Congress complied.

Research Projects

Summarize Abraham Lincoln's early life including where he was born, educated, worked, and lived. Explain how he became involved in politics and how he finally became president.

The situation was dangerous. A large Union army was rampaging through Tennessee and the Army of the Potomac was advancing upon Richmond. In the summer, under the command of Lee, the Confederates had driven the Union army out and had invaded Maryland, while in the West Bragg had invaded Kentucky. The work of Davis and his cabinet seemed to be satisfactory.

The winter of 1862 was harsh for the South, and the inadequacies of its infrastructure led to food shortages, while cotton could not be exported because of the Union blockades.

By March 1863 the military had been empowered to seize private property for repayment at fixed prices. Inflation was running away unchecked, tax had increased, and when the South lost at Gettysburg and Vicksburg, it looked as though all the sacrifices had been for nothing. By the autumn of 1864 the Confederacy was all but bankrupt. As Vice President Stephens remarked: "What good is independence, if the South must sell its very soul to secure it?" Lee had been pushed back to Richmond and Petersburg, Sherman was in the

Carolinas, chasing the Confederates, and all that was left by way of assets were the slaves.

On November 7, 1864 Davis asked Congress for the money to purchase 40,000 slaves, proposing to use them in a non-combatant role within the army, after which time they would be given their freedom. This was the first, very belated step towards Southern emancipation, and both Davis and Robert E. Lee were convinced that salvation for the South lay in taking this course. Congress thought they meant slave soldiers, but Davis wrote emancipation into the orders implementing the law.

So clearly slavery in the South had run its course – brought to an end by an absolute need. The Confederacy lasted a while into 1865; Davis fled from Richmond on April 2 and kept on running when he heard of Lee and Johnston's surrenders. He still hoped to defy Lincoln and Washington, and still harbored desires to lead an insurgent force against the Union. But the South would no longer oblige; it had had enough.

Davis was finally captured at Irwinville, Georgia, on May 10, 1865, by a detachment of Union cavalry. The Confederate States of America had lost their first and only president.

OPPOSITE: Jefferson Davis and his Cabinet.

RIGHT: Jefferson Davis.

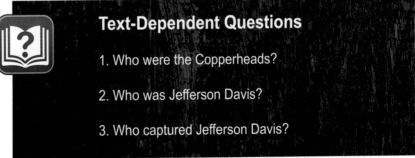

Text-Dependent Questions

1. Who were the Copperheads?

2. Who was Jefferson Davis?

3. Who captured Jefferson Davis?

Chapter Two
BEHIND THE LINES

Even though daily life in the North had been hardly touched by the war, there was no initial shortage of recruits for the Union army. There had been an enormous surge of **patriotism** and Lincoln's original call for 75,000 volunteers had been far exceeded by overzealous state governors. In fact, the Union had suffered something of a crisis, its army support systems being woefully

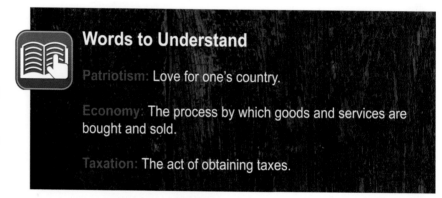

Words to Understand

Patriotism: Love for one's country.

Economy: The process by which goods and services are bought and sold.

Taxation: The act of obtaining taxes.

OPPOSITE and ABOVE: Camp of the 50th Regiment, Pennsylvania Infantry, at Gettysburg.

inadequate; on the one hand it had a surfeit of volunteers, but on the other, there was a lack of uniforms, equipment, and boots. In storage were some 300,000 muskets, but most of them were obsolete models, often as much as 50 years old.

However, the initial wave of patriotism soon faltered, when it was realized that the War Department was unable to ensure its soldiers were properly fed. Soldiers' Aid associations sprang up to collect supplies and distribute them to the troops, but this was never going to be a long-term solution. All was chaos and Washington seemed unable to suggest a viable way forward.

Matters became even more serious after May 3, 1861, when Lincoln asked for an additional 42,000 men, expecting them to serve for three years.

By now the state arsenals were empty, rifles and muskets were hard to come by and they were expensive to buy. The arms manufacturers in the North could produce no more than around 5,000 weapons per month, and the North needed ten times as many.

The situation was no better in the South and gradually both Union and Confederate purchasing agents began to travel the world, looking for new sources of weapons. They were able to buy freely from both the British and the French, but these new weapons would take time to manufacture and ship to the United States. As an interim measure, weapons that

ABOVE: Officers of the 80th New York Infantry "Alston Guard," Culpeper, Virginia.

ABOVE RIGHT: Lieutenant Vane of the Army of the Potomac, Petersburg, Virginia.

had been superseded by new issues were brought out of mothballs by the Belgians, the Prussians, and the Austrians. The Confederacy would continue to rely on imported firearms, but by the spring of 1862 manufacturers in the North had stepped up production and were able to fulfill demand.

It was not only the infantry that suffered from a lack of supply. Although the South had plentiful equipment for its horses, so that it could easily form cavalry and artillery regiments, what was lacking on both sides were carbines, revolvers, and sabers. The states each had complements of artillery pieces, so for the most part, supply of these weapons was not a general concern.

The Confederacy would, however, suffer from a distinct lack of horses, particularly after traditional horse-rearing areas had fallen to Union forces. Thereafter, any available horse was pressed into action.

Both the Union and the Confederacy needed to ensure a steady supply of new recruits for their armies. Mass rallies were held and the Union offered bounties as rewards. The problem, as in most wars, was that civilian wages had increased, due

primarily to the fact that fewer laborers were now available, which did not make the army or navy particularly strong attractions. Moreover, farms had lost many of their casual laborers and farmers were keen to hold onto their sons. It soon became clear, particularly to the North, that volunteers and drafts alone were not going to supply enough troops; the Confederacy first, and then much later the Union, would have to resort to conscription.

For the North there was the problem of what became known as bounty jumpers. Men would sign up, receive their state and Federal bounties and then promptly desert. Then, under an assumed name, they would present themselves to another recruiting officer, collect the bounties again and move on. There were also those who specialized in substitute brokering, substitutes being acceptable if an individual could find another man willing to take his place. This was a practice found in both the North and the South; once the Union army began to accept black

ABOVE: Between the Lines
William Gilbert Gaul (1855–1919).
Oil on canvas.
Private Collection.

OPPOSITE: William T. Sherman at Federal Fort No. 7, Atlanta, Georgia, September–November, 1864. Photographed by George N. Barnard, who produced the best documentary record of the war in the West.

troops, substitute brokers found an almost bottomless pit of potential income.

Conscription was far better organized in the South: after all, there were far fewer men and it was far more difficult to evade the draft. The South, of course, was at a distinct manpower disadvantage, while the North was able to conscript, equip, train, and deploy almost a million men over a three-year period. With this enormous army at its disposal,

however, the North faced considerable problems in organizing it and making sure the necessary resources were supplied when required.

The South, of course, was far less developed in terms of industry and was highly dependent on imports. Stringent measures were taken to ensure that cash crops, such as cotton, were not grown in preference to food. By 1863 the Confederates had gone as far as demanding that farmers donate

BELOW: The devastation of war, Charleston, South Carolina.

OPPOSITE ABOVE: Ruins of a paper mill in Richmond, Virginia.

OPPOSITE BELOW: Buildings destroyed by fire, Richmond.

ten percent of all of their food crops to the armed forces, in spite of which there were still enormous shortages. But by 1863, certainly in terms of food, the South had become practically self-sufficient.

Just as Northern civilians did not suffer greatly during the Civil War, with the exception of those affected by occupation, so standards of living were at least stable for a time. But as the war continued, it became increasingly difficult to obtain manufactured goods. Tea and coffee were hard to find, though basic staples, such as pork, bacon, molasses, and cornmeal, were always available.

As more men were recruited into the army the shortfall in manpower behind the lines had to be replaced. The old, children and women were therefore obliged to work the farms, particularly in the

South, for it should be remembered that the vast majority of the South population did not have slaves of their own.

The center of the Confederacy was Richmond, a place with industrial capacity and formerly many workers. Due to its geographical location, however, it was becoming increasingly difficult to get supplies into the city, causing the cost of living to rise dramatically, and even prompting bread riots. The Confederacy's paper money became increasingly worthless, as shops and traders began to demand payment in gold or silver, a far more stable form of currency. By 1864 it was not unusual to be paying 1,200 Confederate dollars for a barrel of flour. Shortages hit

OPPOSITE: Surrender of a Confederate Soldier, 1873
Julian Scott (1846–1901).

ABOVE: Encampment 1884
Julian Scott (1846–1901).
Painted from photograph taken in Winchester, Virginia in 1862. Possibly "Stonewall" Jackson and Jeb Stewart together?

the South in many different ways, including the restricted printing of newspapers. There, few books were printed, though in the North many newspapers and magazines were published each week.

As for the civilians during the American Civil War, particularly those in remote locations, the carnage of the conflict hardly touched them at all. Increasingly, however, civilians in the South

were faced with a total disruption of their way of life as increasingly large numbers of Union troops began to forge deep into the Southern states. Now they could expect their homes to be looted, their possessions stolen or burned, their horses taken and, of course, in relevant cases, their slaves freed. Similar dangers pertained in the border states and the areas through which the armies marched

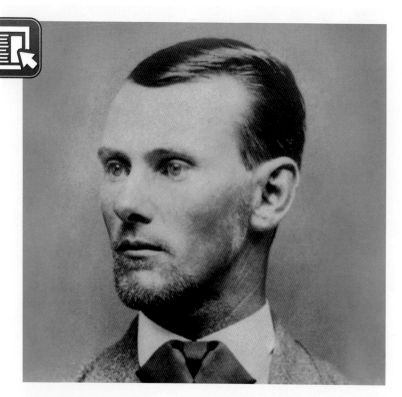

JESSE WOODSON JAMES (1847–1882)

Jesse James was born on September 5, 1847, in Kearney, Missouri. Jesse came from a respected family of farmers. When he was 16 he and his brother Frank joined the Confederate army as guerrilla soldiers or bushwhackers riding along side William Quantrill and "Bloody Bill" Anderson. Some historians accuse the brothers of participating in atrocities committed against Union soldiers, including the Centralia Massacre, but others argue that brutality towards them turned them to a career in crime. After the war, as members of various gangs of outlaws, they robbed banks, stagecoaches, and trains.

The brothers were most active as members of their own gang from about 1866 until 1876, when as a result of their attempted robbery of a bank in Northfield, Minnesota, several members of the gang were captured or killed. There is speculation that the brothers and their gangs were Robin Hood figures, robbing from the rich and giving to the poor. Their crime spree carried on for several years, recruiting new members when required, but were under increasing pressure from law enforcement. On April 3, 1882 Jesse James was killed by Robert Ford, another gang member who hoped to collect a reward on James' head. Famous while alive, James became even more legendary after his death and one of the most memorable figures of the wild west.

and fought. When Lee launched his invasion of the North, which culminated in Gettysburg in July 1863, his troops, like many, lived off the land and took whatever they could find.

There were other examples of men hell-bent on bringing the war to peaceful civilian communities. Even though William Quantrill was an Ohio schoolteacher, he nevertheless joined the ranks of the Confederacy, recruiting a large contingent of mounted raiders, which included Frank and Jesse

ABOVE: Frank James, the brother of Jesse.

OPPOSITE: Haxall's House, which was commandeered as a military hospital after the Battle of White Oak Swamp.

James. Quantrill's raiders attacked Union towns and villages, gunning any man down who got in their way, as well as burning and looting. Quantrill's reign of terror came to an end in May 1865, when at just 27 years of age, he was ambushed by Union cavalry, wounded and later died.

The American Civil War claimed four percent of the entire American male population. Many of the deaths could have been avoided, had there been better medical facilities or, indeed, the North and South had paid some attention to the care of prisoners-of-war. Andersonville in Georgia

was a notorious Confederate prisoner-of-war camp, originally intended to house 10,000 prisoners, but by the summer of 1864 32,000 had been incarcerated, crowded together in squalid conditions. Around 13,000 men alone died due to complete neglect, leading the commander of

RIGHT: In June 1862 Federal Soldiers hung Dr. Rueben Samuels, the step-father of Jess and Frank James in retaliation for their time spent with Quantrill's raiders.

the prison, Henry Wirtz, to be charged with murder and hanged on November 10, 1865.

By 1862 the war was costing the North alone $2.5m per day, which necessitated a vast injection of cash into the economy. The Northern **economy** geared itself to soaking up this surfeit of money; factories built cannons, muskets, and engines, while farmers stepped

up their production of grain and meat. In fact, farm productivity increased significantly.

The Northern textile industry had been stockpiling raw cotton since before the war, but the demand for uniforms was enormous and even these huge resources had become depleted by 1862, causing many of the mills to close down, and forcing

ABOVE: Reading the death warrant to Henry Wirtz, November 1865, Washington D.C. Wirz was the only Confederate soldier to be executed for war crimes in the aftermath of the Civil War.

OPPOSITE: Prisoner-of-war camp at Andersonville, Georgia, in 1864. A south-westerly view of the stockade showing the deadline.

200,000 people out of work.

Unemployment, however, was of no great concern, because the army was desperate for manpower and every business was losing skilled workers every day to conscription. Many of the manufacturers, however, profited from the shortage of cotton, processing rags and raw wool to make poor-quality uniforms that

Research Projects

The Civil War was costly and many lives were lost. Explain and summarize how the war affected agriculture and industry of the South.

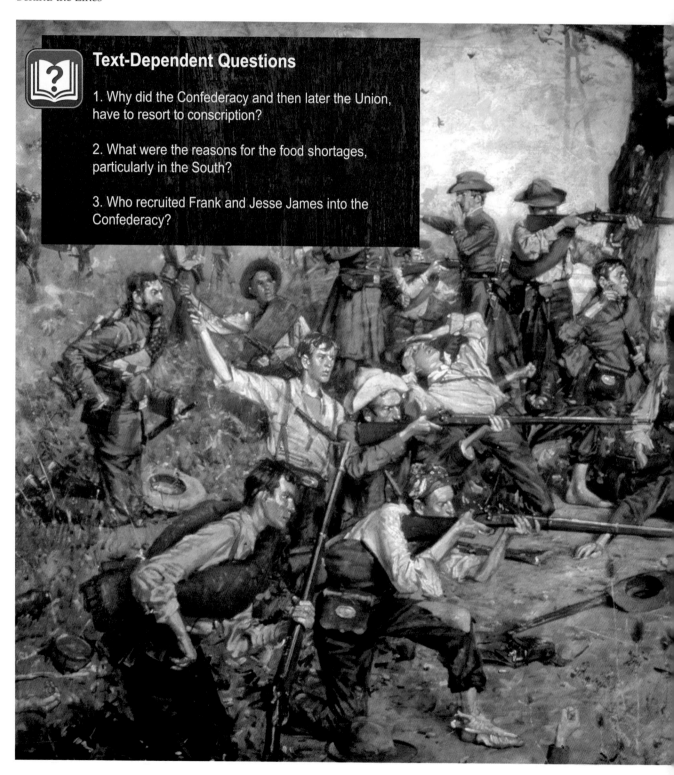

Text-Dependent Questions

1. Why did the Confederacy and then later the Union, have to resort to conscription?

2. What were the reasons for the food shortages, particularly in the South?

3. Who recruited Frank and Jesse James into the Confederacy?

LEFT: Holding the Line at All Hazards
William Gilbert Gaul (1855–1919).
Oil on canvas.

BELOW: The Union Army Advances on a Parapet, Manned by Quaker Guns and Empty Uniforms
Julian Scott (1846–1901).

fell apart within weeks. The North, in particular, imported huge amounts of wool from Britain and Australia and this had developed into a flourishing market by the beginning of 1863. Northern mills had found a new source of raw cotton in India, but were also able to obtain increasing amounts from the Union-occupied Southern states.

Paying for the war proved to be problematical for both the North and the South, neither of them being in favor of heavy **taxation**. As far as the Union was concerned, bank loans funded the first year of the war. The North decided to take the dollar off the gold standard and in February 1862 $150m of paper money was made legal tender, though not redeemable for gold or silver. Eventually, the Northern government would circulate $450m in paper money and at one point a dollar was only worth 35 cents-worth of gold.

The Confederates also produced paper money but did not make it legal tender, with the effect that the Confederate dollar was virtually worthless: even when the Union dollar was worth 35 cents, it was still worth eight times that of the Confederate dollar. The overall cost of the war for the South requires two calculations. Firstly the war itself cost upwards of $600m in gold, while, on top of this, the emancipation of the slaves wiped out another $3bn.

Chapter Three
EMANCIPATION

The American Civil War did not begin as a struggle to end slavery, but as a struggle to preserve the Union. Having said that, it was the most important event in African-American history.

The short-term results of the eventual Union victory meant immediate freedom for upwards of 4 million people, while the egalitarian nature of the 13th and 14th amendments to the **Constitution** would eventually

Words to Understand

Constitution: The system of beliefs and laws by which a country, state, or organization is governed.

Liberation: The act of freeing someone from another's control.

Ku Klux Klan: An American secret society advocating white supremacy

ensure civil rights for the entire black population of the United States.

The fundamental differences of opinion on the issue of slavery are apparent from a remark made by the Vice President of the Confederate States of America, Alexander H. Stephens, speaking in 1861: "Our Confederacy is founded on the great truth that slavery – subordination to the superior race – is [the Negro's] natural and normal condition. Thus, our new government is the first in the history of the world based upon this great physical and moral truth."

Lincoln had originally found himself in something of a quandary regarding emancipation. He is quoted as saying "if slavery is not wrong, nothing is wrong," yet his primary aim was to preserve the Union and the Union permitted slavery.

Lincoln faced opinions from every side on the issue of abolition. Ardent abolitionists implored him to use his war powers to end slavery (which he did in the end), but against this was the fear that he would drive the four border slave states into the arms of the Confederacy. There was considerable anti-black feeling in the North, and both old-fashioned Republicans and Democrats were set against abolition. Lincoln knew that if he acted too soon, the

OPPOSITE: Reading the Emancipation Proclamation.
Library of Congress

RIGHT: Frederick Douglass.

ALEXANDER H. STEPHENS (1812–1883)

Alexander Hamilton Stephens was born on February 11, 1812 to Andrew Baskins Stephens and Margaret Grier. He was raised on a farm in Taliaferro County, Georgia. Although a frail child, Stephens worked hard through the years, eventually taking up legal studies, passed the bar in 1834, and then became a successful lawyer. Stephens was Confederate vice president throughout the American Civil War. His cornerstone speech of March 1861 defended slavery in the most hard-line of terms, though after the war he tried to distance himself from his earlier position. During the course of the war, he became increasingly condeming of Confederate President Jefferson Davis's policies, especially conscription and the suspension of *habeas corpus*. After his arrest for his part in the rebellion, he was released and served in Congress, being elected Governor of Georgia shortly before his death.

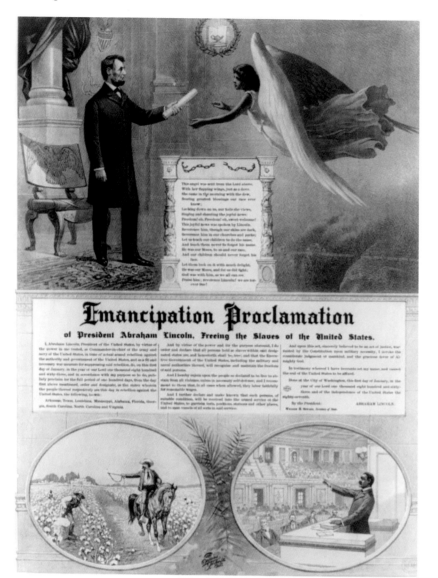

he had already decided to make a proclamation of emancipation, but for the time being at least, he held back, waiting for the right moment. Regardless of Lincoln's own views on slavery, and the pressures exerted on him by the abolitionists, there were very practical reasons to abolish slavery. As the South itself admitted, its economy and culture were wedded to slavery. There were 3.5 million slaves in the 11 Confederate states and without them the Confederacy would have collapsed in a matter of months. Not only did the slaves produce

LEFT: The Emancipation Proclamation.

ABOVE: General Benjamin F. Butler of the Union army.

OPPOSITE: General Butler's Headquarters.

South would fully unite against him, and the North would be divided on the issue, and he could afford neither of these things to happen. In his own words, Lincoln summed up the predicament in which he found himself: "My paramount object in this struggle is to save the Union, and is not either to save or destroy slavery." These words were written to the ardent abolitionist, Horace Greeley, in August 1862 and Lincoln went on to say: "If I could save the Union without freeing any slave I would do it; and if I could save it by freeing all the slaves I would do it; and if I could save it by freeing some and leaving others alone, I would also do that."

Lincoln was not exactly telling the truth, however. At this stage,

the food and cash crops, they were also a source of vital manpower elsewhere. Slaves manned the transportation networks, dug trenches and fortifications, worked in industry, and ensured the Confederate armies were kept regularly supplied. From the very first day of the Confederacy, the reliance on slave labor had been paramount and this would continue to be the case.

The black abolitionist, Frederick Douglass, also noted the reliance of the South on its slave labor, and saw it as the primary reason why Lincoln should endorse the call for abolition: "Why does our government allow its enemies this powerful advantage? The very stomach of this rebellion is the Negro in the condition of a slave. Arrest that hoe in the hands of the Negro and you smite the rebellion in the very seat of its life. To fight against slaveholders, without fighting against slavery, is but a half-hearted business, and paralyses the hands engaged in it."

they were considered to have made a direct contribution to the continuance of the rebellion against the Union.

But emancipation was slowly moving forward. In 1862 the Union forbade officers to return slaves to their owners, and slavery was abolished in the District of Columbia and in all Union territories, while another Confiscation Act in July freed all slaves belonging to those in rebellion against the United States. The final step for Lincoln relied on there being a crushing Union victory on the battlefield, and to this end he would have to prove beyond all doubt that the tide of the war was moving in the Union's direction. His opportunity came at a little-known location called Antietam on September 17, 1862, when the Union army of 90,000 men clashed with almost 60,000 Confederates. The battle ended in a painful, bloody stalemate, but the Union army held and inflicted heavy losses on the Confederates. Although not an outright and striking victory, it proved for the time being that the Union army could hold the Confederates.

LEFT: Commemorative print of President Abraham Lincoln with the text of the Emancipation Proclamation of January 1, 1863
Published in 1865.

OPPOSITE: A Southern View. A depiction of President Abraham Lincoln as the devil, writing the Emancipation Proclamation trampling the U.S. Constitution; demons around him Adalbert J. Volck, 1864.

As Union armies plunged into the South, pro-slavery Union officers returned slaves to their owners, under the terms of the Fugitive Slave Act, while other officers, who were against slavery, looked for ways to save them. In May 1861 General Benjamin Butler of the Union army came up with a novel solution: fugitive slaves, in his view, should be classed as contraband of war. In other words, because they contributed to the economy of the South they should be confiscated. This was ratified as policy in August 1861 with the passing of the Confiscation Act. Henceforth, all property, slaves included, would be seized by the North if

Lincoln issued the preliminary Emancipation Proclamation on September 22, 1862, which did not free a single individual. Moreover, the final proclamation, made on January 1, 1863, that stipulated that all slaves in states in rebellion against the Union would be "forever free," was, in reality, still without substance. The task of freeing the slaves, apart from those who had already fled to the North, would be down to the Union army. From now on, the sight of soldiers in blue, marching through Southern towns and villages, could only mean one thing to the black population – liberation.

There were still those who thought it advisable for freed blacks to leave the United States, and there had been a botched attempt at colonization in August 1862. Lincoln asked for $60,000 to fund a project for 450 freed slaves to be settled in Haiti, but what with financial scandals, smallpox, and starvation, the project failed. Black and white would somehow have to learn to live together as free men.

The approximate wartime population of blacks in the Northern states was 225,000, of which all were freed men, women and children. There were another 500,000 in the four border slave states, and upwards of another half a million who had fled from the South to cross into Union-held territory. This last group had had a mixed reception, but food was provided and schools were established with the help of

OPPOSITE: Antietam Bridge (Burnside's Bridge).

BELOW: Destroyed bridge at Harper's Ferry.

abolitionists. Most significant was the desire of the men to join the Union forces, so that they could fight for the freedom they had so recently won.

At least 200,000 black men served in the Union army and navy, some three-quarters of this total being ex-slaves, the balance being freed black men from the Northern states. Lincoln was reticent on the subject of raising black regiments. In fact he refused to allow Indiana to raise two black regiments for fear of alienating the border states. As one Washington official tactlessly remarked: "Negroes – plantation Negroes, at least – will never make soldiers in one generation. Five white men could put a regiment to flight." Lincoln himself had remarked in September 1862: "If we were to arm these I fear that in a few weeks the arms would be in the hands of the rebels."

Lincoln, Washington officials and other Northern doubters need not have concerned themselves, however. Black soldiers, almost to a man, were not only more willing to drill and learn to be soldiers, they were also more willing to

stand and fight. For them, concepts such as the Union and its preservation were irrelevant. This was a war of **liberation** and the Confederacy had to be swept aside in order to achieve that goal.

As it turned out, pro-abolitionist officers had already been recruiting, one of the recruits being a Massachusetts man,

Thomas Wentworth Higginson. This meant that the first regiments were ready by August 1863, when some 14 were created. Prior to this the 1st South Carolina Volunteers, a prototype black regiment, had already acquitted itself well in South Carolina and Georgia.

Meanwhile, a pair of black Louisiana regiments had been

ABOVE: The battlefield of Antietam on the actual day of the battle.

OPPOSITE: A cavalry orderly at Antietam.

blooded against Confederate positions at Port Hudson, Louisiana, on the Mississippi river, as early as May 1863, leading a white officer of one of the regiments to comment: "You have no idea how my prejudices with regard to Negro troops have been dispelled by the battle the other day."

A fortnight later, an untried black regiment held off a concerted Confederate attack at Milliken's Bend on the Mississippi river. The Union's Assistant Secretary of State watched the action: "The bravery of the blacks completely revolutionized the sentiment of the army with regard to the employment of Negro troops. I heard prominent officers,

**LEFT: Battle of Fredericksburg,
December 13, 1862**
Thure de Thulstrup (1848–1930).
Lithograph.

who formerly in private had sneered at the idea of Negroes fighting, express themselves after that as heartily in favor of it."

On July 16, 1863 it was the turn of the 54th Massachusetts, led by its young colonel, Robert Gould Shaw. The 54th had been the first black regiment to be raised in the North. Eager to prove his men's worth, Shaw and his regiment volunteered to lead the attack on Fort Wagner,

defending the approach to Charleston. Shaw was killed and his regiment suffered heavy losses, but even the Confederates could not deny their bravery. The *New York Tribune* stated after the blood repulse: "It made Fort Wagner such a name to the colored race as Bunker Hill has been for ninety years to the white Yankees." (In fact black soldiers had fought at Bunker Hill, though at the time their presence was not known.)

ABOVE: Camp of the Tennessee Colored Battery, Johnsonville, Tennessee.

OPPOSITE ABOVE: Antietam National Battlefield Memorial, Sharpsburg, Maryland.

OPPOSITE BELOW: Company E, 4th U.S. Colored Infantry at Fort Lincoln, Washington, D.C.

By August 1863 both Lincoln and the pre-eminent Union commander, General Grant (the future president), were convinced that black troops were an integral part of the solution, capable of delivering a mortal blow to the South, both literally and in a wider sense. He told those who still opposed emancipation: "You say you will not fight to free Negroes. Some of them seem willing to fight for you. There will be some black men who can remember that, with silent tongue, and clenched teeth, and steady eye, and well poised bayonet, they

Research Projects

The Emancipation Proclamation was an executive order issued by President Abraham Lincoln on January 1, 1863. Explain its immediate impact and political impact on slavery.

ABOVE: Camp of a Tennessee Colored Battery.

RIGHT: Picket station of colored troops stationed near Dutch Gap, Virginia, 1864.

have helped mankind on this great consummation; while I fear, there will be some white ones, unable to forget, with malign heart, and deceitful speech, they have strove to hinder it."

As the Union infiltrated the Southern territories, more blacks presented themselves as recruits to the Union army. By October 1864 there were no fewer than 140 black infantry regiments, and

significantly, some 38 of these took part in the invasion of Virginia in 1864, and were the first to march into Charleston and Richmond. By the time the war ended, upward of nine percent of

the total enrolment in the Union army had been black men, who would fight in nearly 40 large pitched battles and over 400 smaller engagements during the war. Around 37,000 lost their lives, many more to disease than to Confederate bullets, cannonballs, or bayonets.

The Confederacy, naturally enough, reacted very badly to the recruitment and deployment of black troops, decreeing that all white officers who led them would be charged with inciting a slave insurrection and be summarily executed. Black soldiers would likewise be hanged if it could be

proven they had killed or wounded a Confederate soldier, while the rest would be returned to slavery. Although actions such as these were not carried through, captured black soldiers could expect a particularly rough time. The key restraining factor, however, was Lincoln's clear statement that if black soldiers or their white officers were executed, he would order the systematic execution of Confederate prisoners.

There were, of course, loose cannons among the Confederate ranks who would simply not accept that black soldiers and their white officers deserved the

same treatment as ordinary soldiers. The most extreme of these was Nathan Bedford Forrest, later a leading figure in the **Ku Klux Klan**. He was a leader of Confederate cavalry during the Civil War, often operating deep behind Union lines, and more often than not was more interested in murder, plunder, and rape than military objectives. His men perpetrated what became known as the Fort Pillow Massacre on April 12, 1864 when, having overrun a Union garrison, he ordered the execution of a large number of captured black infantry.

Nonetheless, the South had begun to realize that black men did indeed make good soldiers. Black soldiers had served for the entirety of the war in Confederate white regiments, primarily as substitutes or armed servants of officers. The vexed question as to why these black men had served to prolong their own slavery has never quite been explained. For many, for good or ill, they saw Southern society as their own society and acted to defend it as any other freed man would do.

Why then, with white men serving in the Confederate army and a far looser control over the

OPPOSITE: An 1885 color poster of the Fort Pillow Massacre designed to keep the memory of the atrocity alive.

BELOW: Another illustration of the massacre of Union soldiers following their surrender at Fort Pillow, April 12th, 1864. Published in 1894.

Text-Dependent Questions

1. How many people were eventually freed from slavery following the Union's victory?

2. When did Lincoln issue the preliminary Emancipation Proclamation?

3. When did African-Americans achieve full civil rights?

millions of slaves, did the slave population of the North not rise up in rebellion? Many explanations have been put forward: some touch on the faithfulness of slaves to their masters, others to the strong powers of local militia, or home guards, operating in the countryside to control the slave population. More feasible, however, is the fact that the bulk of the slaves simply did not know what was happening. They were totally unaware not only of the Emancipation Proclamation, but also of the progress of the Union army; this was because a great many lived on plantations or in isolated rural communities where news rarely penetrated.

When Union troops were close at hand, however, they would have seen the home guards flee and their masters burying their valuables in the fields before running away. Then, with the certain knowledge of liberation, they would have headed for the blue-coated soldiers and gained their freedom.

The American Civil War is often referred to as the second American Revolution, in that it swept aside slavery and created four million more citizens of the United States. Had it not been for the thousands of courageous black soldiers in the Union army, and their stalwart determination to win and be counted as men, the Union may never have developed as it did after the Civil War.

The freedom and the civil rights that black soldiers and their white compatriots had won for themselves was eventually to be enshrined in the United States Constitution. Even though the African-American population did not achieve full civil rights until 90 years later, in the 1950s, the contribution they made towards the preservation of the Union can never be underestimated.

Chapter Four
EUROPE AND THE WAR

The dominant power in the world at the time of the American Civil War was the British Empire. Both the Union and the Confederate States of America knew that whatever Britain did, the rest of the world would follow. Despite Britain's power, and its own decision to abolish slavery 30 or so years earlier, it was not about to be coerced into taking sides in the American Civil War.

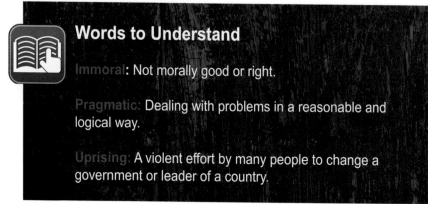

Words to Understand

Immoral: Not morally good or right.

Pragmatic: Dealing with problems in a reasonable and logical way.

Uprising: A violent effort by many people to change a government or leader of a country.

The North was more outspoken when it came to outside intervention, the U.S. Secretary of State, William Seward, intimating, by way of veiled threats, what would happen if Britain or another European power gave the South its support. Seward was rabidly anti-British, and the British, in turn, considered him unscrupulous, **immoral**, and unreliable, treating his remarks as little more than hot air. Lincoln, on the other hand, had a far more pragmatic approach, in that he believed Britain to have no desire to be the ally of either side.

Seward had had the temerity to order European statesmen not to receive Confederate Commissioners. Fortunately for the North, Seward's lack of experience and finesse had been tempered by the presence of Charles Adams, the son of John Quincy Adams, who was the Union's minister in London. Adams was able to diffuse many difficult situations, but the North would not allow the Europeans to openly support the Confederacy, knowing that the Europeans secretly favored the South.

Support for the Confederacy in Britain came from many factions, from Quakers to Roman Catholics, and all believed the

OPPOSITE: General Lee and his Confederate officers in their first meeting since Appomattox, August 1869. This is the only from life photograph of Lee with his Generals in existence, during the war or after.

WILLIAM H. SEWARD (1801–1872)

Appointed by Abraham Lincoln, William Henry Seward was Secretary of State from 1861 to 1869, and earlier served as Governor of New York and United States Senator.

North was suppressing the South. In political circles, the Tories backed the South and found staunch allies among the radicals and the liberals, while in society at large, titled members of the House of Lords through to the leaders of the working classes all favored the Confederate cause. The underlying problem had been a statement in which Lincoln had clearly indicated that the Civil War was not against slavery, but a war to preserve the Union, making it more natural that those

Seward was a leading anti-slavery campaigner in the years leading up to the Civil War, he was a dominant figure in the Republican Party in its formative years, and was generally praised for his work on behalf of the Union as Secretary of State during the Civil War. Seward also carefully negotiated the purchase of Alaska in 1867. Seward was born in Florida, New York, where his father, a farmer, owned slaves. He became educated as a lawyer, moving to the town of Auburn, New York. Seward was elected to the New York State Senate in 1830 as an Anti-Mason. Four years later, he became the Whig Party's gubernatorial nominee, but was unsuccessful. Seward was elected governor in 1838, winning a second two-year term in 1840. During this period he carried on with his important work advancing the rights for black citizens. Seward was also involved in Mexican affairs from 1865 to 1887. Seward died in his hometown of Auburn, New York on October 10, 1872.

fighting for their independence should be supported.

The Confederates earnestly believed that Britain, whose industrial heart was the cotton industry, would have to break the Union blockade or face economic disaster. Southern cotton was essential to Britain, and by the winter of 1862/63 the shortages had begun to bite and over 200,000 British workers were without work. Around half a million people were directly affected by the Union blockade that prevented cotton from reaching Britain.

France was no less affected, in that it obtained 90 percent of its raw cotton imports from the Southern states. It also had pro-Confederate sympathizers who were in favor of giving irect military aid to the Confederacy. But the French emperor, Napoleon III, was terrified at the prospect of siding with the Confederate States of America, especially if Britain remained neutral.

Britain ultimately found other sources of raw cotton, so the shortage was short-lived. In the meantime there was money to be made from manufacturing weapons and ships. The sad fact is that the South did not really have a foreign policy and it was never able to clear the first hurdle – that of being recognized as independent from the Union. This would prove disastrous and allow the Europeans to sit out the war, removing the risk to them

of choosing the wrong side as their ally.

The spring of 1861 had seen some hope for the South. Both Britain and France had recognized the Union as a "belligerent." This was an important step and inferred that they did not accept that the Union was engaged in an internal fight, but was acting against another country. These were the first signs that Europe was coming round to the idea of the South as an entity separate from the United States. Seward was enraged and it seemed that, for a while, his ravings would tip the balance and Britain would indeed side with the South. All the signs were there that Britain would first recognize the Confederacy and then offer it actual assistance in resisting the North.

The flames of war were fanned in November 1861 when two Confederate commissioners, James Murray Mason and John Slidell, headed for Britain, hoping to secure recognition for the

Confederate States of America. They boarded the British ship *Trent*, but the following day, in contravention of international law, Captain Charles Wilkes of the U.S. vessel *San Jacinto* boarded the *Trent* and ordered it to be searched, when he seized the two men. The British demanded an apology for the outrage and the immediate release of Mason and Slidell; even Seward recognized it had been a step too far, and Lincoln concurred; consequently, the North had no choice but to capitulate or face certain and drastic repercussions from the British.

Wilkes was hung out to dry, forced to take the blame for the incident. The two men were released, but this had been the closest the British would ever come to throwing their weight behind the Confederacy.

There was still a hope of this happening following the Second Battle of Bull Run (Manassas) in August 1862, but Britain saw the turning of the tide and decided to remain neutral.

In 1864 Napoleon III of France threw his hat into the ring in the desperate hope of reliving the successes of his uncle, Napoleon Bonaparte. Archduke Maximilian of Austria, having been approached by Mexican monarchists, allowed himself to be persuaded by Napoleon III into becoming Emperor of Mexico.

Theoretically, Napoleon III had acted at the right moment: the American Civil War precluded military intervention by the Union and the South had offered him support in return for recognition.

The plan was short-lived, however; before long, there was a popular **uprising** in Mexico, led by Benito Juárez, and the Emperor Maximilian was executed.

As the Union began to amass victories towards the end of the Civil War, so it had become more vociferous in its protests against French involvement in Mexico. On the one hand the Union feared the French would militarily support the South, but it could not intervene itself. In the end French troops withdrew from Mexico and left Maximilian to his fate.

In the end, the South's attempts to gain recognition and help from Europe came to nought. Great Britain remained neutral, as did France and Prussia, and even the Spanish, with hopes of holding onto their Caribbean possessions, kept out of the conflict. Sweden, Belgium, and the Vatican also failed to act, having waited in vain for leadership to come from Great Britain.

The Russian Tsar, Alexander II, had even refused to see the Confederate envoys. Russia had little need of American manufactured goods or food and in fact saw a strong, united America as a useful force with which to constrain Britain.

What concerned Britain and France most were the possible losses inflicted on them by the Union blockade, though in reality their vessels were constantly breaking them. The French wanted harbors to be free of blockade, but the North would not agree. As a consequence, many British and French vessels worked as privateers, which was an effective way of getting goods in and out of the South.

Confederate ships were built in both British and French ports, Liverpool being a prime example; it provided at least 70 blockade-runners to the South between 1862

OPPOSITE LEFT: James Murray Mason.

OPPOSITE RIGHT: John Slidell.

ABOVE: The *Alabama* with the *Brilliante* in the background.

Research Projects

Summarize how other countries viewed the Civil War.

and 1865, some of which were crewed by British sailors, while others were sold direct to the Confederacy. The *Alabama*, *Florida* and *Shenandoah*, warships that preyed on Northern shipping, were also supplied by Britain to the Confederacy, as were ironclad rams, though these were bought outright by the Royal Navy as a safeguard against Union protests.

Neither the Union nor the Confederacy could have hoped to have waged war without the masses of muskets built in Britain and shipped across the Atlantic in vast numbers. The Enfield model, used by both sides in huge quantities, was either manufactured in Britain or made

OPPOSITE: The Battle of the Kearsage and the Alabama, 1864
Édouard Manet (1832–83).
Oil on canvas.

BELOW: Lt. Col. James J. Smith and officers of the 69th New York Infantry (Irish Brigade).

Text-Dependent Questions

1. Why did Britain tend to sympathize with the Confederacy in the early years of the war?

2. Who did France sympathize with in the early years?

3. Why did Britain and France remain neutral in the later years?

under license in the United States.

Another considerable contribution to the American Civil War was the enormous flow of immigrants, who continued to arrive despite the conflict. Between 1861 and 1863 alone, 180,000 Irish arrived in the United States, while a conservative estimate of 100,000 enrolled in the Union army. In fact, virtually all Irish regiments flourished, including the famous Irish Brigade of the Union army.

In fact, men from all over Europe could be found in the ranks of the Confederate armies, some, of course, being

adventurers, while others were fighting for their own perceptions of liberty and independence.

In the end it was not the bluster and threats of the North that ensured Europe's neutrality. Britain, in particular, had taken a cautious and **pragmatic** view, having various interests in other parts of the world that required its attention. But this tended to work in the Union's favor; even though the Union had failed to win European support, by working to ensure that Europe did not support the South, the Union had gained more freedom to deal with the rebellion in its own way

TIME LINE OF THE CIVIL WAR

1860

November 6
Abraham Lincoln elected president.

December 20
South Carolina secedes from the Union, followed two months later by other states.

1861

February 9
Jefferson Davis becomes the first and only President of the Confederate States of America.

March 4
Lincoln sworn in as 16th President of the United States.

April 12
Confederates, under Beauregard, open fire on Fort Sumter at Charleston, South Carolina.

April 15
Lincoln issues a proclamation calling for 75,000 volunteers.

April 17
Virginia secedes from the Union, followed by three other states, making an 11-state Confederacy.

April 19
Blockade proclamation issued by Lincoln.

April 20
Robert E. Lee resigns his command in the United States Army.

July 4
Congress authorizes a call for half a million volunteers.

July 21
Union forces, under McDowell, defeated at Bull Run.

July 27
McClellan replaces McDowell.

November 1
McClellan becomes general-in-chief of Union forces after the resignation of Winfield Scott.

November 8
Two Confederate officials are seized en route to Great Britain by the Union navy.

1862

February 6
Grant captures Fort Henry in Tennessee.

March 8–9
The Confederate ironclad *Merrimac* sinks two Union warships, then fights the *Monitor*.

April 6–7
Confederates attack Grant at Shiloh on the Tennessee river.

April 24
Union ships under Farragut take New Orleans.

May 31
Battle of Seven Pines, where Joseph E. Johnston is badly wounded when he nearly defeats McClellan's army.

June 1
Robert E. Lee takes over from Johnston and renames the force the Army of Northern Virginia.

June 25–July 1
Lee attacks McClellan near Richmond during the Seven Days' Battles. McClellan retreats towards Washington.

July 11
Henry Halleck becomes general -in-chief of the Union army.

August 29–30
Union army, under Pope, defeated by Jackson and Longstreet at the Second Battle of Bull Run.

September 4–9
Lee invades the North, pursued by McClellan's Union army.

September 17
Battle of Antietam. Both sides are badly mauled. Lee withdraws to Virginia.

September 22
Preliminary Emancipation Proclamation issued by Lincoln.

November 7
McClellan replaced by Burnside as commander of the Army of the Potomac.

December 13
Burnside decisively defeated at Fredericksburg, Virginia, 1863.

1863

January 1
Lincoln issues the final Emancipation Proclamation.

January 29
Grant assumes command of the Army of the West.

March 3
U.S. Congress authorizes conscription.

May 1–4
Hooker is decisively defeated by Lee at the Battle of Chancellorsville. Stonewall Jackson is mortally wounded.

June 3
Lee invades the North, heading into Pennsylvania.

June 28
George Meade replaces Hooker as commander of the Army of the Potomac.

July 1–3
Lee is defeated at the Battle of Gettysburg.

July 4
Vicksburg – the last

Confederate stronghold on the Mississippi – falls to Grant and the Confederacy is now split in two.

July 13–16
Draft riots in New York

July 18
54th Massachusetts, under Shaw, fails in its assault against Fort Wagner, South Carolina.

August 21
Quantrill's raiders murder the inhabitants of Lawrence, Kansas

September 19–20
Bragg's Confederate Army of Tennessee defeats General Rosecrans at Chickamauga.

October 16
Grant given command of all operations in the West.

November 19
Lincoln gives his famous Gettysburg Address.

November 23–25
Grant defeats Bragg at Chattanooga.

1864

March 9
Grant assumes command of all armies of the Union. Sherman takes Grant's old job as commander in the West.

May 5–6
Battle of the Wilderness.

May 8–12
Battle of Spotsylvania.

June 1–3
Battle of Cold Harbor.

June 15
Union troops miss a chance to capture Petersburg.

July 20
Sherman defeats Hood at Atlanta.

August 29
Former General McClellan becomes the Democratic nominee for president.

September 2
Atlanta is captured by Sherman.

October 19
Sheridan defeats Early's Confederates in the Shenandoah Valley.

November 8
Lincoln is re-elected president.

November 15
Sherman begins his March to the Sea.

December 15–16
Hood is defeated at the Battle of Nashville.

December 21 Sherman reached Savannah in Georgia.

1865

January 31
Thirteenth amendment approved to abolish slavery.

February 3
Peace conference between Lincoln and Confederate vice president fails at Hampton Roads, Virginia.

March 4
Lincoln inaugurated as president.

March 25
Lee's last offensive is defeated after four hours at Petersburg.

April 2
Grant pushes through Lee's defensive lines at Petersburg. Richmond is evacuated as Union troops enter.

April 4
Lincoln tours Richmond.

April 9
Lee surrenders his army to Grant at Appomattox Courthouse, Virginia.

April 10
Major victory celebrations in Washington.

April 14
Lincoln shot in a Washington theater.

April 15
Lincoln dies and Andrew Johnson becomes president.

April 18
Confederate General Johnston surrenders to Sherman in North Carolina.

April 19
Lincoln's funeral procession.

April 26
Lincoln's assassin, Booth, is shot and dies in Virginia.

May 23–24
Victory parade held in Washington.

December 6
Thirteenth Amendment approved by Congress. It is ratified and slavery is formally abolished.

BELOW: Statue of Thomas "Stonewall" Jackson at Gettysburg National Military Park.

Educational Videos about the American Civil War

The Gettysburg Address
A speech by U.S. President Abraham Lincoln, one of the best-known in American history. It was delivered by Lincoln during the American Civil War, on the afternoon of Thursday, November 19, 1863, at the dedication of the Soldiers' National Cemetery in Gettysburg, Pennsylvania.

Everyday Animated Map
A useful video explaining how the Union and Confederate armies gained ground through the various battles.

"Dear Sarah," A Soldier's Farewell to his Wife
A Civil War soldier's heartbreaking farewell letter written before his death at Bull Run.

The War Between the States
Historian Garry Adleman gives an overview of the causes, campaigns, and conclusion of the Civil War.

History, Key Figures, and Battles
A useful, concise dramatized, video explaining the American Civil War.

EXAMPLES OF CONFEDERATE UNIFORMS

Robert E. Lee in his general's uniform

Trooper, Stuart's Cavalry Corps.

Infantry Soldier

Marines

Virginia Cavalry

Louisiana
Tigers

Georgia
Infantry

4th Alabama
Regiment

South
Carolina
Regiment

Engineer

73

EXAMPLES OF UNION (FEDERAL) UNIFORMS

Ulysses S. Grant in his general's uniform

Indiana Regiment

5th New York Volunteers

39th New York Voluntry Infantry Regiment

Iron Brigade of the U.S.

U.S. Marine Corps

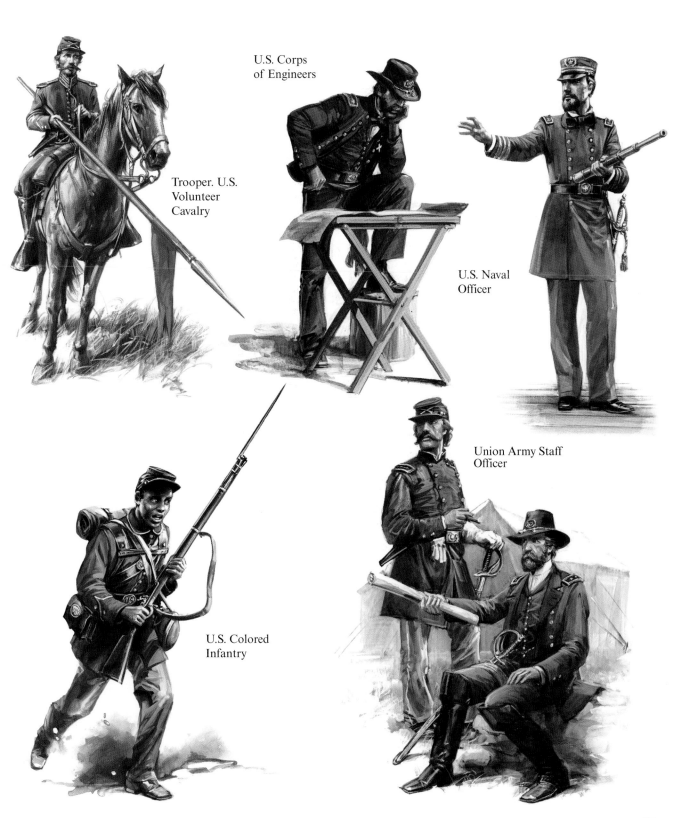

Trooper. U.S.
Volunteer
Cavalry

U.S. Corps
of Engineers

U.S. Naval
Officer

Union Army Staff
Officer

U.S. Colored
Infantry

Series Glossary of Key Terms

Abolitionist A person who wants to eliminate slavery.

Antebellum A term describing the United States before the Civil War.

Artillery Large bore firearms like cannons and mortars.

Assassination A murder for political reasons (usually an important person).

Cash Crop A crop such as cotton, sugar cane, or tobacco sold for cash.

Cavalry A section of the military mounted on horseback.

Confederacy Also called the South or the Confederate States of America. A term given to 11 southern states seceding from the United States in 1860 and 1861.

Copperhead A person in the North who sympathized with the South during the Civil war.

Dixie A nickname given to states in the southeast United States.

Dred Scott Decision A decision made by the Supreme Court that said Congress could not outlaw slavery.

Emancipation An act of setting someone free from slavery.

Gabion A basket filled with rocks and earth used to build fortifications.

Fugitive Slave Law A law passed by Congress in 1850 that stipulated escaped slaves in free states had to be retured to their owners.

Infantry Soldiers that travel and fight on foot.

North The states located in the north of the United States, also called the Union.

Plantation An area of land especially in hot parts of the world where crops such as cotton and tobacco are grown.

Slavery The state of a person who is owned or under the control of another.

Secession Withdrawal from the Federal goverment of the United States.

Sectionalism A tendency to be concerned with local interests and customs ahead of the larger country.

South The states located in the south of the United States, also called the Confederacy.

Union The name given to the states that stayed loyal to the United States.

West Point The United States Military Academy.

Yankee A nickname given for people from the North and Union soldiers.

Further Reading and Internet Resources

WEBSITES

http://www.civilwar.org

http://www.historyplace.com/civilwar

http://www.historynet.com/civil-war

www.britannica.com/event/American-Civil-War

BOOKS

Bruce Catton. *The Centennial History of the Civil War,* Doubleday, 1962. Kindle edition 2013.

Ulysses S. Grant. *The Complete Personal Memoirs of Ulysses S.* Grant Seven Treasures Publications, 2009

James Robertson and Neil Kagan. *The Untold Civil War: Exploring the Human Side of War.* National Geographic, 2011.

If you enjoyed this book take a look at Mason Crest's other war series:

The Vietnam War, World War II, Major U.S. Historical Wars.

Index

PHOTOGRAPHIC ACKNOWLEDGEMENTS

All images in this book are supplied by the
Library of Congess/public domain and under license
from © Shutterstock.com other than the following:
Regency House Publishing Limited: 7, 72-73, 74-75.

The content of this book was first published as
CIVIL WAR.

ABOUT THE AUTHOR
Johnathan Sutherland & Diane Canwell
Together, Diane Canwell and Jonathan Sutherland are
the authors of 150 books, and have written
extensively about the American Civil War. Both
have a particular interest in American history, and its
military aspects in particular. Several of their books
have attracted prizes and awards, including New York
Library's Best of Reference and Book List's
Editor's Choice.